# Keep Calm
# and
# Trust God

BY
JAKE PROVANCE
&
KEITH PROVANCE

*Keep Calm and Trust God*
ISBN: 978-1-939570-15-4
Copyright © 2014 by Word and Spirit Publishing

Published by Word and Spirit Publishing
P.O. Box 701403
Tulsa, Oklahoma 74170

Creative concept by Ryan Provance

# Table of Contents

# Introduction

The British government coined the slogan "Keep Calm and Carry On" in 1939 as the threat of World War II loomed. In the event that Hitler's army invaded England, the posters were to be distributed to England's general population in an effort to galvanize their resolve to resist German aggression. Should Germany invade across the English Channel, it would be one of the darkest times in world history.

Under the shadow of Nazi air raids and bombing runs, death and destruction, and a world thrown into chaos, the British knew the people would need encouragement. The future of the free world teetered in the balance. And in those dark times, believers everywhere prayed fervently.

Thankfully, most of us will never have to face that kind of tragedy and adversity in our own lives. Nevertheless, today we find ourselves embroiled in a different kind of war.

Our lives seem to be under constant assault. Worry, fear, stress, and anxiety make war on many of us daily. Our society has accepted depression and discouragement as common social ailments. Anxiety threatens to immobilize us, as unfulfilled dreams, loss, divorce, sickness, death, failures, mistakes, and criticism seem to rain down on us like bombs.

But God is not the author or cause of such destructive atrocities. The Bible clearly states in John 10:10 that it is Satan that is the enemy who comes to steal, and to kill, and to destroy. Jesus came that we might have life—and life more abundantly.

So where do we turn in these trying times? The same place the Christians in World War II did: prayer.

Just as with the British facing the threat of German invasion, we must "Keep Calm and Carry On." When adversity comes, however, simply keeping calm is not enough. We cannot fight the enemy of our soul with a slogan. Nor can we "carry on" in our own strength. We need to rely on and gain our strength from God. We need to trust Him completely and totally.

Whether we realize it or not, many of the battles we face in our lives today are spiritual battles, and we cannot win with just our own willpower. When trouble comes your way or when bad news hits you right between the eyes, be determined to replace fear with confidence in God, to replace worry with faith in Him, and to replace anxiety with His peace. Keep calm, and most of all, trust God.

God has promised to never leave you or forsake you. He wants to be a part of your life. When you need His help, all you have to do is ask. In your hour of greatest need, He will uphold you and sustain you. He will give you peace in the midst of the storms of life.

Our hope is that the following pages will provide encouragement, strength, and inspiration to overcome whatever challenges you may be facing in your life. God is on your side; God is for you! He will see you through!

"The beginning of anxiety is the end of faith, and the beginning of true faith is the end of anxiety."

—GEORGE MUELLER

# Anxiety

Anxiety seems to be all around us, all the time. Sometimes, just the normal hassles of daily living can cause us to be anxious. Anxiety can steal our ability to enjoy friends, family, and life in general. Anxiety can contribute to high blood pressure, stomach or intestinal disorders, and heart attacks. It can even lead to panic attacks or nervous breakdowns.

Sure, life is full of challenges, conflicts, and stressful situations, but we don't have to let them produce anxiety in our lives. Whatever the cause or source, anxiety serves no good purpose. Life is too short to allow anxiety to steal the joy of living a peaceful, productive, and fulfilled life!

God provides the key to combating anxiety in Philippians 4:6-7: "Do not be anxious about anything, but in every situation, by prayer and petition, with thanksgiving, present your requests to God. And the peace of God, which transcends all understanding, will guard your hearts and your minds in Christ Jesus" (NIV).

That pretty much sums it up—prayer with thanksgiving produces peace. And not just any peace, but a supernatural peace that comes from God and that surpasses all human understanding! Isn't that good news?

Jesus said in John 14:27, "Stop allowing yourself to be anxious and disturbed: and do not permit yourself to be fearful and intimidated and cowardly and unsettled" (AMP). Based on that, Jesus must be telling us that living an anxiety-free life is a *choice*.

You can choose to rise above anxiety. Put your trust in God and refuse to be discouraged and agitated. Count your blessings! Put your confidence in Him, for He loves you, cares for you, and believes in you.

## Prayer

*Lord, help me not to be anxious. I know that, whatever I am facing, you are right there with me and have promised to never leave me or forsake me. Help me to trust you despite the circumstances that surround me. Lord, when I am tempted to be anxious, help me to speak your promises, to overcome the attacks on my mind with answers from your Word. Let me be quick to respond to wrong thoughts and desires by replacing them with good thoughts.*

*Thank you, Lord, that you light the way before me. You give me clear instruction and keep me firmly on the paths of righteousness. I put my complete trust in you. You are my shield and my refuge. You are my rock and my fortress. You are my hiding place and strong tower. In the midst of the storm, you enlighten me with your understanding and give me your peace. I refuse to be anxious about anything.*

## Scriptures

Humble yourselves, therefore, under God's mighty hand, that he may lift you up in due time. Cast all your anxiety on him because he cares for you. Be self-controlled and alert. Your enemy the devil prowls around like a roaring lion looking for someone to devour.

—1 PETER 5:6-8 (NIV)

Do not fret *or* have any anxiety about anything, but in every circumstance *and* in everything, by prayer and petition (definite requests), with thanksgiving, continue to make your wants known to God. And God's peace [shall be yours, that tranquil state of a soul assured of its salvation through Christ, and so fearing nothing from God and being content with its earthly lot of whatever sort that is, that peace] which transcends all under-standing shall garrison *and* mount guard over your hearts and minds in Christ Jesus.

—PHILIPPIANS 4:6-7 (AMP)

We shall steer safely through every storm, so long as our heart is right, our intention fervent, our courage steadfast, and our trust fixed on God. If at times we are somewhat stunned by the tempest, never fear, Let us take breath, and go on afresh.

—FRANCIS DE SALES

"Worry implies that we don't quite trust God is big enough, powerful enough, or loving enough to take care of what's happening in our lives."

—FRANCIS CHAN

# Worry

We all face the daily opportunity to worry about something—our health, finances, family, jobs, the economy. The list is endless. If we let them, our worries can consume our lives!

Yet worry is so unproductive, it accomplishes nothing except producing anxiety, stress, and fear. Worry will rob you of your joy, peace, and faith. It can cloud your mind and often leads to irrational thinking.

Worry's strength and hold on your life only grows if you dwell on your problems. But there is great news—God's plan is for you to live a worry-free life! You may be wondering, *How is that possible?* Simple: by putting your complete trust and confidence in God and His Word. God promised that He would never leave you or forsake you, and the Bible tells us in Matthew 6:25 not to worry about your life.

If you were to look through the eyes of your Heavenly Father, you would see that no situation or circumstance is too great for God! Our problems are actually quite small compared to how big our God is!

The secret so many people miss is that it's not enough to tell yourself not to worry about something; you have to *replace* worried thoughts with God's thoughts. When you dwell on the Word, you dwell on His thoughts. Paul refers to this process as "renewing your mind" in Romans 12:2. Making it a part of your daily routine to read, meditate, and speak God's Word will transform your life!

When worry tries to grip you, tell yourself to keep calm and trust God, because He is going to take care of you. You are more precious than gold to Him!

## Prayer

*Lord, help me not to worry about anything. I am looking to you to see me through this situation. In obedience to your Word, I cast all my care, concern and worry on you. Grant me your peace to remain steady and calm. Help me to let your peace rule and reign in my heart.*

*I put my trust and confidence in you. I know you love me and care for me as a loving Father. I know you will not let me down. I believe you are working everything out for my good. Lord, reveal to me your perfect will in this situation. Let me keep looking to you and not let my heart be troubled or fearful. Help me to be spiritually strong and courageous and not to let my emotions or feelings dictate my actions.*

## Scriptures

Therefore I tell you, do not worry about your life, what you will eat or drink; or about your body, what you will wear. Is not life more than food, and the body more than clothes? Look at the birds of the air; they do not sow or reap or store away in barns, and yet your heavenly Father feeds them. Are you not much more valuable than they? Can any one of you by worrying add a single hour to your life?

—MATTHEW 6:25-27 (NIV)

Cast thy burden upon the LORD, and he shall sustain thee: he shall never suffer the righteous to be moved.

—PSALM 55:22

What shall we then say to these things? If God be for us, who can be against us?

—ROMANS 8:31

"Worry does not empty tomorrow
of its sorrow, it empties today of
its strength."

—CORRIE TEN BOOM
(HOLOCAUST SURVIVOR)

"I learned that courage was not the absence of fear, but the triumph over it. The brave man is not he who does not feel afraid, but he who conquers that fear."

—NELSON MANDELA

# Fear

Fear may be your greatest enemy. It can steal your joy, rob your peace, and paralyze your faith. It can dull your senses, confuse your mind, and produce irrational thoughts and behavior. Fear can cause us to say and do things we would never even consider under normal circumstances.

Fear takes on many forms. It can show up as a small dread or as a paralyzing and crippling force that renders us helpless mentally, physically, and spiritually. Whatever its manifestations, it's essential that we recognize that fear is a spiritual force that can negatively affect our lives and can only be conquered by a greater spiritual force—our faith in God.

Jesus frequently told people to "fear not." He recognized the devastating effect that fear can have on our faith. Fear can stop the blessings of God from flowing into our lives. It's God's will for us to live a fear-free, faith-filled life every day. If Jesus told us to "fear not," then that means we have the capability to do it. Did you know that "fear not" or variations of the phrase like "do not be afraid" occur 365 times in the Bible? That's one for every day of the year!

But how do we put that directive into practice? We fight fear with our faith. And we activate our faith with our *words*.

When fear tries to come against you, you resist it with your words. Say out loud, "Jesus has not given me a spirit of fear, but of power and love and a sound mind. I will not be afraid because Jesus said not to. I will remain calm and trust the Lord. *I will not fear*."

## Prayer

*Lord, help me not to be afraid, because you are with me. Show me how to think on good things and not on things that will produce fear. Fear is an enemy of my heart and mind, and I refuse to let it steal the peace and joy in my life.*

*Give me courage and strength to face the fears in my life that try to hold me captive. You have assured me you would remain with me in times of trouble and comfort me when fear grips my heart.*

*I choose to trust in you instead of fear. You uphold me and sustain me. Let me have your peace and wisdom and when I am tempted to fear I will look to you. You have made me secure, capable and free from fear in my life. I am fearless.*

## Scriptures

So do not fear, for I am with you; do not be dismayed, for I am your God. I will strengthen you and help you; I will uphold you with my righteous right hand.

—ISAIAH 41:10 (NIV)

Have not I commanded thee? Be strong and of a good courage; be not afraid, neither be thou dismayed: for the LORD thy God is with thee whithersoever thou goest.

—JOSHUA 1:9

The LORD is my light and my salvation; whom shall I fear? the LORD is the strength of my life; of whom shall I be afraid?

—PSALMS 27:1

For God hath not given us the spirit of fear; but of power, and of love, and of a sound mind.

—2 TIMOTHY 1:7

# The Arena

"It is not the critic who counts; not the man who points out how the strong man stumbles, or where the doer of deeds could have done them better. The credit belongs to the man who is actually in the arena, whose face is marred by dust and sweat and blood; who strives valiantly; who errs, who comes short again and again, because there is no effort without error and shortcoming; but who does actually strive to do the deeds; who knows great enthusiasms, the great devotions; who spends himself in a worthy cause; who at the best knows in the end the triumph of high achievement, and who at the worst, if he fails, at least fails while daring greatly, so that his place shall never be with those cold and timid souls who neither know victory nor defeat."

—Theodore Roosevelt

"Depression is a prison where you are both the suffering prisoner and the cruel jailer."

—DOROTHY ROWE

# Depression

Depression is your enemy. It can steal your joy and peace. It can become a cloud that casts a shadow over everything in your life. Depression dulls your senses and causes you to view every area of life through a dark filter. It can take you down a road of despair and discouragement that only leads to worry, fear, and hopelessness.

Some say that depression is a natural response to adverse events or circumstances in our lives. Maybe it seems that way in your life right now, but it doesn't have to be that way forever! Did you know that you can choose *not* to be depressed? You can choose to take control of your life back from depression. Find your joy in the Lord instead of living "up" one day and "down" the next. Choose to live by faith instead of letting the circumstances of life dictate how you feel.

It is not God's will for you to be discouraged, down, and depressed. You can choose to be joyful even in the midst of the most difficult situations.

Fight back against depression! Go on the offensive with your thoughts and your words. What are you thankful for? Count your blessings. Go to the Bible and look up scriptures on encouragement and begin to speak them over your life. No matter what situation you find yourself in, you can find something to be thankful for. This is the key to the prison of depression.

God loves you, and He knows what you are going through. He wants to help you. Go to Him in prayer. Cast your cares on Him, because He cares for you and desires you to live a happy, joyous, and fulfilled life.

## Prayer

*Lord, help me to overcome depression. I know there is no problem too big, no hurt too deep and no mistake so bad that you cannot provide power, strength and wisdom to overcome it.*

*Give me courage and strength to conquer this depression. Restore my joy and help me to trust you. I cast my cares and worries on you because you care for me. I refuse to let depression control my life.*

*Help me to replace my fears with faith, my doubts with belief, my worries with trust and my lack of confidence with courage. Show me how to think the right things and to focus on you and not on my problems. Help me to be thankful for all the things you have provided in my life.*

*Lord, help me to encourage myself in you. Let your joy be my strength and your peace fill my soul. Let your grace and mercy comfort and sustain me.*

DEPRESSION

## Scriptures

Why am I discouraged? Why is my heart so sad? I will put my hope in God! I will praise him again—my Savior and my God!

—PSALM 42:11 (NLT)

I waited patiently for the LORD; he inclined to me and heard my cry. He drew me up from the pit of destruction, out of the miry bog, and set my feet upon a rock, making my steps secure. He put a new song in my mouth, a song of praise to our God. Many will see and fear, and put their trust in the LORD.

—PSALMS 40:1-3 (ESV)

Friends, when life gets really difficult, don't jump to the conclusion that God isn't on the job. Instead, be glad that you are in the very thick of what Christ experienced. This is a spiritual refining process, with glory just around the corner.

—1 PETER 4:12-13 (MSG)

## Don't Quit

"When things go wrong, as they sometimes will;
When the road you're trudging seems all uphill;
When the funds are low and the debts are high;
And you want to smile but you have to sigh.
When all is pressing you down a bit-
Rest if you must, but don't you quit
Success is failure turned inside out;
The silver tint on the clouds of doubt;
And you can never tell how close you are;
It may be near when it seems far.
So stick to the fight when you're hardest hit –
It's when things go wrong that you must not quit."

—JOHN GREENLEAF WHITTIER

Lord, when we long for life without difficulties, remind us that oaks grow strong in contrary winds and diamonds are made under pressure.

—PETER MARSHALL

# Pressure

We all have to deal with various pressures in our lives: pressure to act, to perform, to conform, to stand out, or to advance. We can even feel pressured to buy things we don't need to impress people we don't know or to fix a troubled marriage or rescue a rebellious teen.

But when the pressure is on, it can distract us so that we don't think clearly. Seldom do we make good decisions or wise choices when we are under pressure. In fact, when you feel the pressure that you have to make a rush decision, that's the very moment when you should back up, take a breath, and *make* yourself take some time to analyze your choices more closely.

The pressures of life can overwhelm us if we let them. So the key is—*don't let them!* When you start to feel the pressure of a situation, turn to God and His Word. The Lord has promised that He will give us wisdom if we will just ask Him.

Refuse to give in to pressure, and instead spend some time in prayer, asking the Lord for wisdom and guidance concerning whatever situation you are facing. It might also be a good idea to get some input from a trusted friend who might have a more objective perspective.

The Bible tells you to cast our cares on God, to trust Him, because He cares for you. He will take what the enemy has meant for evil and turn it into good. With every temptation and pressure, God has promised relief and a way of escape. Refuse to let the pressures of life steal your joy and peace.

## Prayer

*Lord, please help me to stay calm and maintain my peace when faced with pressured situations. Help me not to feel forced into making rash or hasty decisions. Show me how to not give in to the pressure to act before I am confident what the correct course of action actually is. Help me not to let the pressure of the moment force me into making an ill-fated decision that I will regret. Give me wisdom and clarity of thought to properly discern the choices available to me. Let me not to be agitated, disturbed or intimidated by the circumstances around me. Grant me your peace so that I may maintain calmness in the midst of adversity. I ask you for your guidance and direction concerning the choices before me. Lord I trust you and will follow your direction.*

## Scriptures

We are hard pressed on every side, but not crushed; perplexed, but not in despair; persecuted, but not abandoned; struck down, but not destroyed.

—2 CORINTHIANS 4:8-9 (NIV)

Consider it a sheer gift, friends, when tests and challenges come at you from all sides. You know that under pressure, your faith-life is forced into the open and shows its true colors. So don't try to get out of anything prematurely. Let it do its work so you become mature and well-developed, not deficient in any way.

—JAMES 1:2-4 (MSG)

And we know that all things work together for good to them that love God, to them who are the called according to His purpose.

—ROMANS 8:28

"We are hedged in (pressed) on every side [troubled and oppressed in every way], but not cramped or crushed; we suffer embarrassments and are perplexed and unable to find a way out, but not driven to despair; We are pursued (persecuted and hard driven), but not deserted [to stand alone]; we are struck down to the ground, but never struck out and destroyed;"

—2 CORINTHIANS 4:8-9 AMP

"When one door closes, another opens; but we often look so long and so regretfully upon the closed door that we do not see the one which has opened for us."

—ALEXANDER GRAHAM BELL

# Regret

We all have regrets. It is practically impossible to live on this earth for any length of time and have no regrets. The trick is to not let regrets have *you,* because if you are not careful, regret can control you.

Maybe you feel your mistakes have been so big that you don't deserve God's help. Welcome to the crowd! None of us *deserve* it, but by His grace, God has made it available to us. Maybe you've done things that have left you feeling ashamed and hopeless. Past sins that make you feel unworthy or failures that make you feel inadequate can hang over your head. Whatever regrets you have, they bar the doorway of your future. Whenever you want to step out for God, regret can stand in your way, laughing at you.

We've all fallen short with our choices and made mistakes. We've all sinned and messed up. But it's time to get back up and brush yourself off.

God does not hold *any* of your past mistakes and failures against you! When you ask God to forgive you, He throws your sins in the sea of forgetfulness and remembers them no more. It's time for you to do the same! If He has forgiven you, don't you think it's time to forgive yourself?

Do your best to learn from the past, but never let the regrets of the past keep you from pursuing your dreams for the future. With God's help, you can rise above your mistakes. Let's face it—mistakes, failures, and missteps are a part of life. But regret doesn't have to be. You are the righteousness of God through Christ Jesus, so it is time to rise again!

## Prayer

*Dear Lord, help me not to worry or have any frustration or anxiety about the mistakes I have made. I cast all the cares and concerns of my past upon You. I forget the past and look toward tomorrow. Let Your peace reside in my heart, in my life and in my home. Today is a new day for me, with no regrets. No matter how many times I stumbled in the past, I can start fresh and new in You.*

*I recognize that no amount of regret can change the past, but I know that You can restore anything that I have lost. I ask You to redeem my mistakes and failures and help me to receive Your forgiveness.*

*I trust You to fulfill Your plans and purposes in my life. Lord, I thank You that You have a bright future planned for me.*

## Scriptures

Brethren, I count not myself to have apprehended: but this one thing I do, forgetting those things which are behind, and reaching forth unto those things which are before.

—PHILIPPIANS 3:13

If we confess our sins, He is faithful and just to forgive us our sins and to cleanse us from all unrighteousness.

—1 JOHN 1:9

"Where is the god who can compare with you—wiping the slate clean of guilt, Turning a blind eye, a deaf ear, to the past sins of your purged and precious people? You don't nurse your anger and don't stay angry long, for mercy is your specialty. That's what you love most. And compassion is on its way to us. You'll stamp out our wrong doing. You'll sink our sins to the bottom of the ocean. You'll stay true to your word...

—MICAH 18-20 (MSG)

# Liberation

When purpose feels questionable,
And you aren't capable,
Your strength fades
As you waver like the field's blades,

Feeling so much to be void of feeling,
Crying tearless staring at the ceiling,
Trapped in a circle of promised change,
While realizing you're poisoned by regret's fang,

There is something you need to hear
Something to spark love's pure tear
Stop trying to run so far,
You're doing better than you think you are,

Jesus came because of His deep love for you.
You matter more than you think you do,
Stop trying to be this and that, just be His
It's less about you than you think it is

—JAKE PROVANCE
INSPIRED BY THE STEVEN FURTICK SERMON
"THE MOST ENCOURAGING MESSAGE YOU'VE NEVER HEARD"

"If you are stressed by anything external, the pain is not due to the thing itself, but to your estimate of it; and this you have the power to revoke at any moment"

—MARCUS AURELIUS

# Stress

In this day and age, we are no strangers to stress. Mental tension and worry caused by our problems—and life in general—can be a hallmark of daily life. Stress can fuel cancer, shrink the brain, age you prematurely, lead to clinical depression, weaken your immune system, and increase the risk of stroke and heart attack. In short, stress is killing us!

And it's not just the big events in our lives that cause us stress. It's the day-to-day grind we put ourselves through. We live in a fast-paced society where it's common to have an overly-busy schedule. Day in and day out, we sacrifice ourselves for our job, our friends, our hobbies, and our family. You may be a student trying to work and go to school, a dad trying to work two jobs to provide for your family, or a stay-at-home mom cleaning the house and taking the kids to school and practices—if stress is killing you slowly, it's time to put on the brakes.

It's not God's will for you to live a life full of stress. The Bible tell us that we can maintain a sense of peace in our lives. So what do we do to break the stress cycle?

Simply starting your day with a morning devotional and a few minutes of prayer can set the tone for a stress-free day. Listening to worship music and meditating on scriptures throughout the day can help you keep your sanity and maintain a peaceful spirit. Try embarking on your day infused with the peace and joy of God in your heart. It will help you to sail right through those potentially stressful situations with ease and grace.

## Prayer

*Lord, help me to live free from stress. Fill me with your peace. Show me how to trust you and be calm, even when the circumstances of my life are screaming so loudly that it's difficult to hear anything else. Let me rise above turmoil and agitation to a place of perfect peace in your presence.*

*By faith, and in obedience to your Word, I cast all my cares, all my anxieties and all my stress on you. I receive your peace in exchange. Help me to focus on you and your Word and not allow stress to affect my life in any way. Show me how to develop a calm spirit and the spiritual strength to not let the cares of this world cause frustration or pressure in my life.*

*I choose to worship you and praise you. I purpose to have a grateful heart, no matter what I am going through. With your help and guidance, I am confident that I can live a stress-free life.*

## Scriptures

Peace I leave with you, my peace I give unto you: not as the world giveth, give I unto you. Let not your heart be troubled, neither let it be afraid.

—JOHN 14:27

Come unto me, all ye that labour and are heavy laden, and I will give you rest.

—MATTHEW 11:28

These things I have spoken unto you, that in me ye might have peace. In the world ye shall have tribulation: but be of good cheer; I have overcome the world.

—JOHN 16:33

If you work the words into your life, you are like a smart carpenter who dug deep and laid the foundation of his house on bedrock. When the river burst its banks and crashed against the house, nothing could shake it; it was built to last.

—LUKE 6:48 (MSG)

Are you tired? Worn out? Burned out
on religion? Come to me. Get away
with me and you'll recover your life.
I'll show you how to take a real rest.
Walk with me and work with me –
watch how I do it. Learn the
unforced rhythms of grace. I won't
lay anything heavy or ill-fitting on
you. Keep company with me and
you'll learn to live freely and lightly.

—MATTHEW 11:28-30 MSG

"Our fatigue is often caused not
by work, but by worry, frustration
and resentment."

—DALE CARNEGIE

# Frustration

Life is full of little daily annoyances and frustrations. There are inconsiderate drivers, fast food drive-through clerks who never get your order right, an endless series of red lights when you're in a hurry, the clueless shopper who takes 45 things to the "10 items or less" checkout register, and on and on.

Maybe you face frustration on a higher level—like feeling as though you're stuck in a dead-end job, or trying to get through to a rebellious teen. Perhaps you're frustrated with yourself because you just can't seem to lose weight or stick with that exercise plan. Maybe you can't find the opportunity to spend quality time with your spouse or kids or you feel you are not on the spiritual level you desire. Whatever the source, frustration can keep you agitated, upset, and just no fun to be around.

The Bible has an excellent weapon to keep frustrations from infiltrating your life. It is maintaining an attitude of gratitude and cultivating a lifestyle of thanksgiving. When you catch yourself starting to get frustrated, start saying out loud, "I refuse to get frustrated, I have a lot to be thankful for." Then begin to say some of the things you are thankful for *out loud*. Your frustration will start to melt away like a snowball in the hot August sun. If it's a problem that needs to be solved, then ask for God's help. He said He would give wisdom to anyone who would ask (see James 1:5).

Refuse to let petty frustrations affect you or steal your joy. Instead, enter into God's presence by giving thanks and praising Him!

## Prayer

*Lord Jesus, help me not to let frustration produce stress and anxiety in my life. Let me be patient with myself and with others. When life is hectic and demanding , show me how to not let frustration rob my peace and steal my joy. Lord, help me to maintain a peaceful spirit and a good attitude even though the circumstances around me are not ideal.*

*When faced with challenges and obstacles in my life, help me face them with a resolute determination. Empower me to press on with confidence, knowing you have promised to give me strength to overcome any situation. When things don't go as expected, let me remain calm, trusting you and not giving in to frustration.*

*Grant me clarity of thought, mental focus and comprehension. Give me wisdom and guidance on how to navigate through the storms of life and arrive at a place of complete victory. I will not be unsettled, distraught or frustrated. Instead, your peace will rule in my life.*

## Scriptures

Understand this, my dear brothers and sisters: You must all be quick to listen, slow to speak, and slow to get angry.

—JAMES 1:19 (NLT)

Let us not lose heart in doing good, for in due time we will reap if we do not grow weary.

—GALATIANS 6:9 (NASB)

The LORD shall fight for you, and ye shall hold your peace.

—EXODUS 14:14

Delight thyself also in the LORD: and he shall give thee the desires of thine heart.

—PSALM 37:4

For I reckon that the sufferings of this present time are not worthy to be compared with the glory which shall be revealed in us.

—ROMANS 8:18

"Our Greatest weakness lies in giving up. The most certain way to succeed is always to try just one more time"

—THOMAS EDISON

"Finish each day and be done with it. You have done what you could. Some blunders and absurdities no doubt crept in; forget them as soon as you can. Tomorrow is a new day. You shall begin it serenely and with too high a spirit to be encumbered with your old nonsense."

—RALPH WALDO EMERSON

# Self-Criticism

So often we can be our own worst enemies. We set unrealistic expectations for ourselves and are critical of ourselves when we don't live up to them. But self-criticism is a destructive process that can undermine what God wants to accomplish in our lives.

It's time to borrow a page from God's playbook and give yourself some grace. We are all works in progress. We all make mistakes, we all drop the ball, and we all fall short. *So what?* When you miss the mark, get up, dust yourself off, and get back in the game.

That's not to make light of the fact that there is always room for improvement, and yes, we should make a habit of evaluating our own lives. Everyone needs to make adjustments at times to get back on track to living a more fulfilled and productive life, but there is a big difference between self-*evaluation* and self-*criticism*. Self-evaluation is a constructive, beneficial exercise that helps us recognize the areas where we need to improve. On the other hand, self-criticism is a destructive force that can lead to discouragement, discontent, and depression.

If we want a change in our lives, then instead of constantly criticizing ourselves and tearing ourselves down, we need to build ourselves up by meditating on and speaking aloud God's Word. God is not in Heaven criticizing you; He is at the head of a great crowd of witnesses cheering you on! God's Word has strength, direction, and promises for you—if you will seek them out. Ask the Lord to help you in areas you need to improve. By His Spirit and through His Word, you can accomplish anything.

## Prayer

*Help me not to be judgmental or condemning toward myself, but to forgive myself just as you have forgiven me. Let me not be critical about my shortcomings. Help me to realize that I am not perfect and never will be, but that's okay. You still love me anyway. Show me how to love myself.*

*Give me grace and mercy to know that I am a work in progress and to be kind to myself. When I make a mistake, help me not to get down on myself. Teach me not to get discouraged or lose heart when I miss the mark. You said you would never condemn me. Help me to follow your example. Teach me to encourage myself in you. Give me confidence to live my life free from self-criticism and condemnation.*

*Continue the good work that you started in me and help me to complete that work in my life.*

## Scriptures

Let no corrupt communication proceed out of your mouth, but that which is good to the use of edifying, that it may minister grace unto the hearers.

—EPHESIANS 4:29

All scripture is given by inspiration of God, and is profitable for doctrine, for reproof, for correction, for instruction in righteousness:

—2 TIMOTHY 3:16

Fight the good fight of the faith. Take hold of the eternal life to which you were called and about which you made the good confession in the presence of many witnesses.

—1 TIMOTHY 6:12(ESV)

Sin is no longer your master, for you no longer live under the requirements of the law. Instead, you live under the freedom of God's grace.

—ROMANS 6:14 (NLT)

"I want you to start a crusade in your life—
to dare to be your best. I maintain that you
are a better, more capable person than you
have demonstrated so far. The only reason
you are not the person you should be is
you don't dare to be. Once you dare, once
you stop drifting with the crowd and face
life courageously, life takes on a new
significance. New forces take shape within
you. New powers harness themselves for
your service."

—EXCERPT FROM *I DARE YOU* BY
WILLIAM DANFORTH

"No one can make you feel inferior
without your consent"

—ELEANOR ROOSEVELT

# Seeking the Approval of Others

We all like to be appreciated. Physiologists tell us that it is one of the greatest desires in every individual. If you are honest with yourself, you will admit that you enjoy being appreciated—we all do. Whether it's a pat on the back from your boss, a handshake of appreciation from your pastor, or a simple "thanks, Mom" from your child for making pancakes for breakfast, we all want to be appreciated. Appreciation provides us with a sense of purpose, and it is one of the most powerful motivators.

But we get into dangerous territory when we begin to rely on the approval of others to determine our self-worth or the level of joy in our life. We can begin to volunteer at church so everyone will see what good Christians we are. We can pray with a little more zeal to show friends how spiritual we are. We can try to be the perfect mom and wife in public so people will notice and recognize our accomplishments. If we are not careful, we may find ourselves doing the right things—for the wrong reasons. If you start viewing your importance, your ability, and your worth the way you think those around you view it, it's time for a change.

If you are constantly seeking the approval of others to determine your happiness, you will find yourself living a very unhappy life. If you put too much emphasis on what others think, you may make decisions based on how you think others will respond, not based on your own purpose, destiny, desires, or God's Word.

Let God remind you who you are in Christ today!

## Prayer

*Lord, help me not to live my life as a people pleaser. Let me have the confidence in myself and in you so I won't have to strive for the approval of others. Grant me the confidence to trust my own heart and instincts.*

*Let my desire and goal be to live my life in such a way that honors you. I choose to conduct my life with integrity and purpose based on the principles of your Word, not on the opinions of others.*

*Help me to be open to the advice and council of others but strong enough to follow my own heart and convictions. Help me not to let the criticism or insults of others offend me or hurt my feelings. Help me to be more sensitive to your guidance and direction than the voices of others. I desire your approval more than the approval of others.*

## Scriptures

Am I now trying to win the approval of human beings, or of God? Or am I trying to please people? If I were still trying to please people, I would not be a servant of Christ.

—GALATIANS 1:10 (NIV)

The fear of man bringeth a snare: but whoso putteth his trust in the LORD shall be safe.

—PROVERBS 29:25

But just as we have been approved by God to be entrusted with the gospel, so we speak, not to please man, but to please God who tests our hearts

—1 THESSALONIANS 2:4 (ESV)

People are illogical, unreasonable, and self-centered
**Love them anyway**
If you do good, people will accuse you of selfish ulterior motives.
**Do good anyway**
If you are successful, you will win false friends and true enemies.
**Succeed anyway**
The good you do today will be forgotten tomorrow
**Do good anyway**
Honesty and frankness make you vulnerable.
**Be honest and frank anyway**
The biggest men and women with the biggest ideas can be shot down by the smallest men and women with the smallest minds.
**Think big anyway**
People favor underdogs but follow only top dogs.
**Fight for a few underdogs anyway**
What you spend years building may be destroyed overnight
**Build anyway**
People really need help but may attack you if you do help them
**Help people anyway**
Give the world the best you have and you'll get kicked in the teeth.
**Give the world the best you have anyway**

—THE PARADOXICAL COMMANDMENTS BY KENT M. KEITH, WAS PROUDLY DISPLAYED IN MOTHER TERESA'S CALCUTTA'S CHILDREN'S HOME

"The greatest mistake you can make
in life is continually fearing that
you'll make one."

—ELBERT HUBBARD

# Fear of the Future

Fear of the future can torment us. It can paralyze us from taking action to prevent the very things we fear most from coming to pass—the "what ifs." *What if I lose my job; what if I get a life-threatening disease; what if my kids make some stupid mistake; what if the economy collapses; what if there is a nuclear holocaust?* The list can go on and on. When you are fighting fears about your future and you need clarity, it's time to turn to God.

Fears about the future may haunt you, but it is not God's will for you to live under that pressure. God has not given us a spirit of fear!

While we can't control what the future holds, we *can* take certain steps to help fashion our future to the image we desire. If we eat right and exercise, we increase the likelihood of having a long life. If we live within our budget and save money, then it is more likely that we can have a retirement without financial burdens.

While it's good to be concerned enough about your future to make wise choices today, don't let your concern turn into worry or fear. Trust God that no matter what happens, He will take care of you. Even if you have made mistakes and wrong decisions, He is merciful and will sustain you and bring you out. Trust in Him, and He will give you peace and clarity. The Bible is God's guide for your life, and it says to trust in the Lord with all your heart and lean not on your own understanding; in all ways acknowledge Him and He will direct your steps.

## Prayer

*Lord, I pray that you would reveal to me the desires and plans that you have for me. Kindle a passion in my heart to pursue the course that you have prepared for me. Send the right people and influences into my life. I trust you with my future.*

*Fulfill your plan and purpose in my life. Help me to be obedient to whatever your will is for my life. Lead, guide and direct my steps. Give me courage and strength to overcome any obstacle that stands between me and the destiny you have for me.*

*Give me patience and persistence. Let me not lose heart or give up when I face setbacks, but be bold and strong in my faith. Give me fortitude to press on when I am tempted to give up and quit.*

*May my life be a testimony of your love, your passion and your abundant provision. In Jesus' name I pray, amen.*

## Scriptures

Be strong. Take courage. Don't be intimidated. Don't give them a second thought because God, your God, is striding ahead of you. He's right there with you. He won't let you down; he won't leave you.

—DEUTERONOMY 31:6 (MSG)

Trust in the LORD with all thine heart; and lean not unto thine own understanding. In all thy ways acknowledge him, and he shall direct thy paths.

—PROVERBS 3:5-6

"For I know the plans I have for you," declares the Lord, "plans to prosper you and not to harm you, plans to give you hope and a future."

—JEREMIAH 29:11(NIV)

For I know the thoughts that I think toward you, saith the LORD, thoughts of peace, and not of evil, to give you an expected end.

—JEREMIAH 1:12

"The sea is dangerous and its storms are terrible, but these obstacles have never been sufficient reason to remain ashore. Unlike the mediocre, intrepid spirits seek victory over those things that seem impossible. It is with an iron will that they embark on the most daring of all endeavors, to meet the shadowy future without fear and conquer the unknown."

—Written in 1520, By the great explorer Ferdinand Magellan

"Obstacles cannot crush me, every obstacle yields to stern resolve, he who is fixed to a star does not change his mind"

—LEONARDO DA VINCI

# Unexpected Setbacks

Setbacks are just part of life. When you receive "setback" news, you will either fall apart or choose to find the good in the situation and trust God. Be careful which one you choose; the second choice is much, much harder than the first, but the payoff is immeasurable.

My family and I had been living in our brand new home for just six days when a fire broke out in the attic. Guests were staying with us, and we were all panicked as we rushed to escape the blaze. Fortunately, everyone made it out safely. We huddled together on the sidewalk and watched the firemen battle the fire. As smoke and orange-red flames poured out of the building, we knew that all of our stuff inside would likely be damaged or lost.

My wife looked at me with tears in her eyes and said, "Okay, mister. What is good about *this?*" I looked around at her, our kids, and our guests—we were all safe and sound. I answered, "What is good about this? Everyone I love is standing on this sidewalk with me!" Sometimes we only see the terrible thing in front of us and don't realize that it could have been something far worse.

What we make of setbacks, how we handle them, and what we choose to do about them defines us and makes us who we are. When you choose to look for the good and you handle setbacks with godly grace, it points people to your source—God!

We may not love disappointments and setbacks, but we also shouldn't hate them. Instead, see them as opportunities to say, "What is good about this?"

## Prayer

*Lord, help me to realize that setbacks are normal to life. Let me not be fearful, anxious or overwhelmed because of this set back, but enable me to lean on you and rely on you and your strength to see me through any situation.*

*Help me not to be discouraged or resentful and not to dwell on the past but to anticipate and look towards the future with hope and expectation.*

*Show me how to turn my setbacks into comebacks. If there are any lessons to learn, reveal to me what I need to know; and then give me guidance and wisdom to go forward with confidence in the pursuit of your plan for my future.*

*I refuse to let setbacks or failures defeat me or define me. I put my trust in you, Lord, and I have confidence you will direct my steps and bring to fruition your plan and purpose for my life.*

## Scriptures

Many are the afflictions of the righteous: but the LORD delivered him out of them all.

—PSALMS 34:19

Being confident of this very thing, that he which hath begun a good work in you will perform it until the day of Jesus Christ.

—PHILIPPIANS 1:6

For a righteous man falls seven times and rises again, but the wicked stumble in times of calamity.

—PROVERBS 24:16 (ESV)

But those who hope in the LORD will renew their strength. They will soar on wings like eagles; they will run and not grow weary, they will walk and not be faint.

—ISAIAH 40:31(NIV)

Abraham Lincoln's many "Setbacks", on his way to his greatest Triumph.

1831 - Lost his job (setback)

1832 - Defeated in run for Illinois State Legislature (setback)

1833 - Failed in business (setback)

- Elected to Illinois State Legislature (success)

1835 - Sweetheart died (setback)

1836 - Had nervous breakdown (setback)

1838 - Defeated in run for Illinois House Speaker (setback)

1843 - Defeated in run for nomination for U.S. Congress (setback)

1846 - Elected to Congress (success)

1848 - Lost re-nomination (setback)

1849 - Rejected for land officer position (setback)

1854 - Defeated in run for U.S. Senate (setback)

1856 - Defeated in run for nomination for Vice President (setback)

1858 - Again defeated in run for U.S. Senate (setback)

1860 - Elected President (success)